Earth WORDS

A Dictionary of the Environment

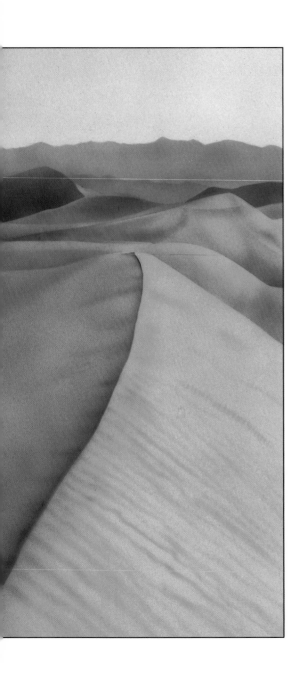

Earth

A Dictionary of

Seymour

illustrated by Mark Kaplan

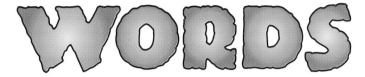

WORDS

the Environment

Simon

HarperCollins*Publishers*

The illustrations in this book were created using gouache, water color, liquid acrylic, and colored pencil on letramax bristol paper.

Earth Words
A Dictionary of the Environment
Text copyright © 1995 by Seymour Simon
Illustrations copyright © 1995 by Mark Kaplan
All rights reserved. No part of this book may be used or reproduced in any manner whatsoever without written permission except in the case of brief quotations embodied in critical articles and reviews. Printed in Mexico. For information address HarperCollins Children's Books, a division of HarperCollins Publishers, 10 East 53rd Street, New York, NY 10022

Library of Congress Cataloging-in-Publication Data
Simon, Seymour
  Earth words: a dictionary of the environment / Seymour Simon ; illustrated by Mark Kaplan.
    p.   cm.
  Summary: Defines words and terms commonly used in discussing the environment, from "acid rain" to "wetland."
  ISBN 0-06-020233-5. — ISBN 0-06-020234-3 (lib. bdg.)
  1. Pollution—Dictionaries, Juvenile. 2. Ecology—Dictionaries, Juvenile.   [1. Ecology—Dictionaries. 2. Pollution—Dictionaries.] I. Kaplan, Mark, date ill. II. Title.
TD173.S56.   1995   92-34005
363.73'03—dc20   CIP
                                                                             AC

1 2 3 4 5 6 7 8 9 10

First Edition

acid rain and snow Rain or snow that becomes highly acid when it mixes with certain gases in the atmosphere, such as sulfur dioxide and nitric oxide. The gases come from power plants that burn high-sulfur fuels, from car exhausts, and from natural sources such as volcanoes and forest fires. Acid precipitation can kill animals and plants that live in water and can damage trees. It can also wear down the bricks and stones of buildings and monuments.

air pollution *See* pollution

atmosphere The air surrounding Earth. The main gases in the atmosphere are nitrogen (78%), oxygen (21%), argon (about 1%), carbon dioxide (0.03%), and small amounts of many other gases. Water vapor, dust particles, smoke, and industrial pollutants are also present in changing amounts. Clouds and weather occur mostly in the bottom 5-to-10-mile layer of the atmosphere, called the troposphere.

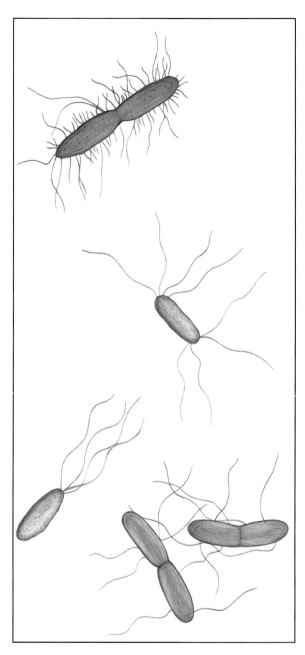

bacteria Tiny, one-celled living things found in soil, water, and air. Some kinds of bacteria can cause disease. Other bacteria break down dead plant and animal materials and help to recycle the nutrients in them.

biodegradable Describes materials such as food wastes and tree leaves that organisms such as bacteria and fungi can easily break down into simpler substances. Many human-made materials, such as plastics, are much less biodegradable.

biological control The use of natural methods to decrease the number of insects or other pests that damage crops. Biological control methods include bringing in other animals to eat insect pests or spreading bacteria that cause disease in the pests.

biome A large community of animals and plants that live together in a region determined by its environment. Biomes include tropical rain forests, deserts, coral reefs, and the arctic tundra.

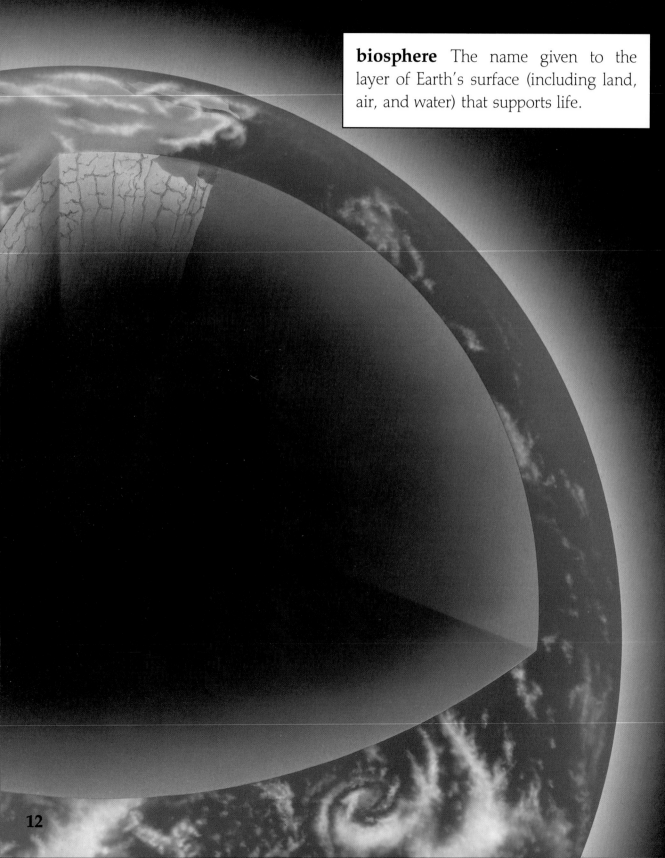

biosphere The name given to the layer of Earth's surface (including land, air, and water) that supports life.

carnivore A flesh-eating mammal such as a tiger, seal, or wolf. Also, an insect-eating plant such as a Venus's-flytrap.

CFC's A group of chemicals (CFC stands for chlorofluorocarbon) once commonly used in refrigerators and air conditioners. Many scientists think it is mainly CFC's that are responsible for the reduction of the ozone layer in the atmosphere. CFC's are slowly being replaced in industry by other chemicals less harmful to the ozone layer.

community A group of plants and animals living and interacting in a small area such as a pond or a forest.

compost The rich dirtlike material left over when worms, bacteria, and fungi decompose (break down) leaves, grasses, and food scraps. Composting is a way to get rid of yard and food waste.

decomposer A living thing such as bacteria or fungi that feeds upon dead plants and animals. Decomposers cause rot and decay and recycle nutrients back into the environment, where they can be used again by living plants and animals.

15

desert A dry region that gets less than ten inches of rainfall (or snowfall) per year. The familiar sandy deserts are found in the very warm areas around the equator. However, there are also deserts in temperate areas, and icy deserts in the Arctic and Antarctic.

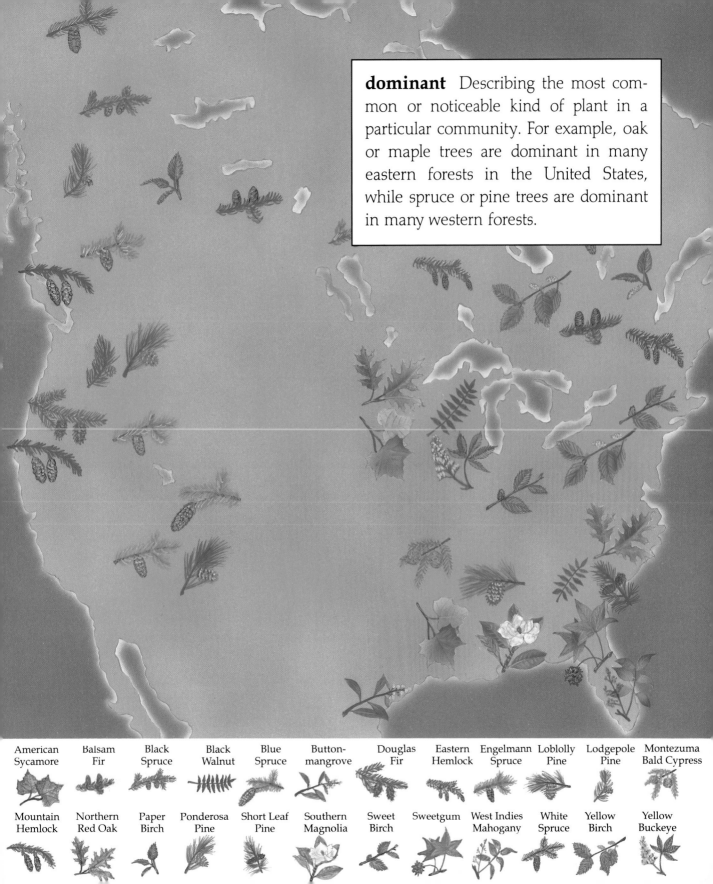

dominant Describing the most common or noticeable kind of plant in a particular community. For example, oak or maple trees are dominant in many eastern forests in the United States, while spruce or pine trees are dominant in many western forests.

American Sycamore

Balsam Fir

Black Spruce

Black Walnut

Blue Spruce

Button-mangrove

Douglas Fir

Eastern Hemlock

Engelmann Spruce

Loblolly Pine

Lodgepole Pine

Montezuma Bald Cypress

Mountain Hemlock

Northern Red Oak

Paper Birch

Ponderosa Pine

Short Leaf Pine

Southern Magnolia

Sweet Birch

Sweetgum

West Indies Mahogany

White Spruce

Yellow Birch

Yellow Buckeye

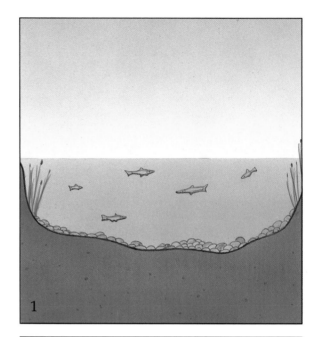

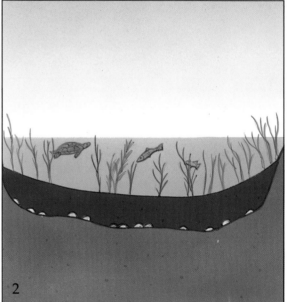

dump A land area where solid wastes are deposited. Most dumps are open areas that do not protect the environment. *See also* landfill.

ecological succession The changes that take place over time in an ecosystem in which the kinds of living things change as conditions change. In barren areas, for example, soil begins to form as rocks weather and break down. Over

3

4

ecology The scientific study of the relationships of living things to one another and to their surroundings.

hundreds of years, different kinds of plants and animals appear and disappear. Finally, a stable ecosystem appears which may last for a long time and is called a climax community.

ecosystem All living things in an area and the physical surroundings in which they live. Ecological systems, or ecosystems, include deserts, fields, forests, ponds, and streams all over the Earth. The combined ecosystems of the world make up the biosphere.

19

California Condor

Green Turtle

Humpback Whale

Redwood Tree

African Elephant

Giant Panda

endangered species An animal or plant, such as the African elephant or the California condor, whose numbers have been so reduced that they may not survive in the wild. Humans can sometimes cause the extinction of a species such as the Atlantic gray whale by too much hunting. They can also endanger many species at the same time by polluting the water or air, or by draining swamps or leveling forests that are the only homes of certain animals or plants.

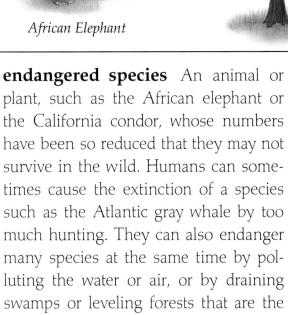

Mountain Gorilla

environment All the surroundings that affect how a living thing develops and survives. The environment includes such factors as weather and climate, sunlight, water, soil, living space, available food, other animals and plants, and the interactions among these things.

erosion The natural weathering or wearing away of land or rock by rain, wind, running water, glaciers, gravity, or living things. Erosion can have harmful effects; when soil is washed or blown away, crops cannot be grown.

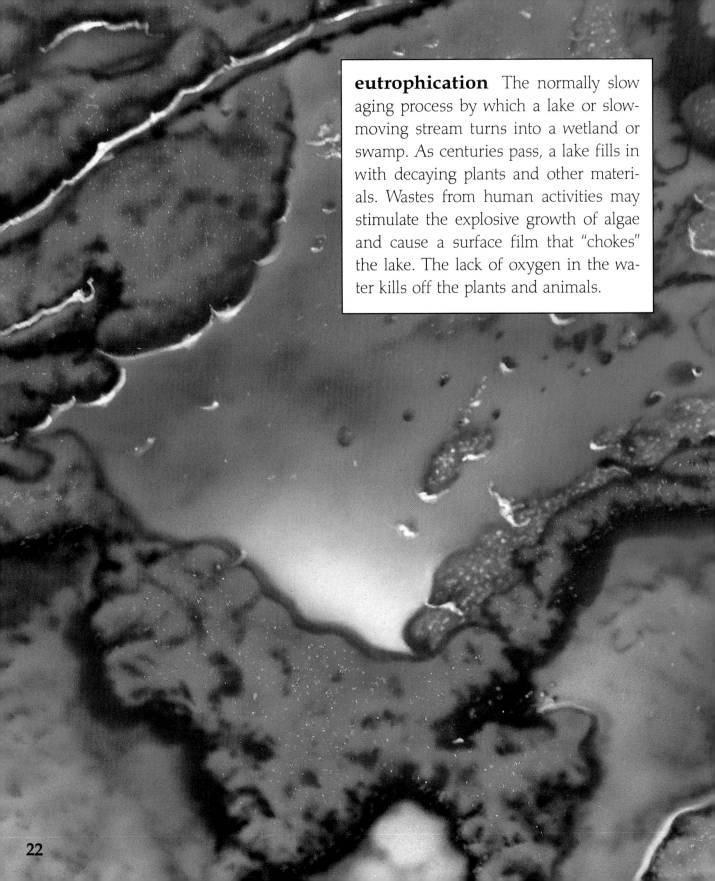

eutrophication The normally slow aging process by which a lake or slow-moving stream turns into a wetland or swamp. As centuries pass, a lake fills in with decaying plants and other materials. Wastes from human activities may stimulate the explosive growth of algae and cause a surface film that "chokes" the lake. The lack of oxygen in the water kills off the plants and animals.

Pteranodon

Tyrannosaurus Rex

Cycad

Woolly Mammoth

Passenger Pigeon

Brachiosaurus

Dodo Bird

extinct Describing a species of animal or plant that no longer exists on earth. Dinosaurs and woolly mammoths are extinct. Some scientists guess that about forty species of plants or animals go extinct each year.

fallout The radioactive dust particles that fall to the ground after a nuclear explosion. Radioactive particles can be carried by winds for great distances before they fall to the surface.

food chain The order in which various animals feed on other plants and animals. A typical food chain starts with green plants, which are eaten by animals called herbivores, which in turn are eaten by other animals called carnivores.

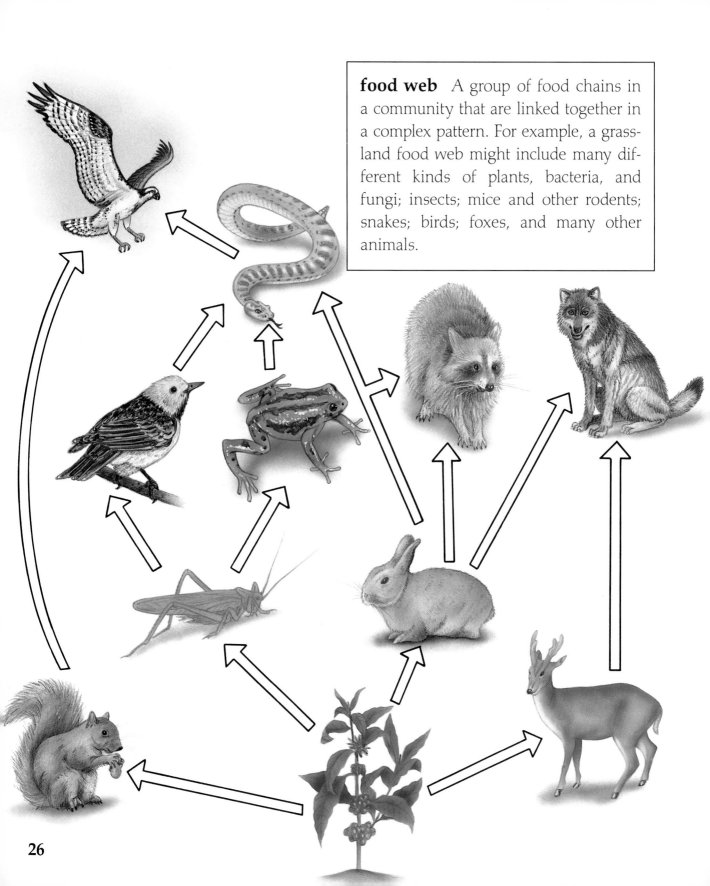

food web A group of food chains in a community that are linked together in a complex pattern. For example, a grassland food web might include many different kinds of plants, bacteria, and fungi; insects; mice and other rodents; snakes; birds; foxes, and many other animals.

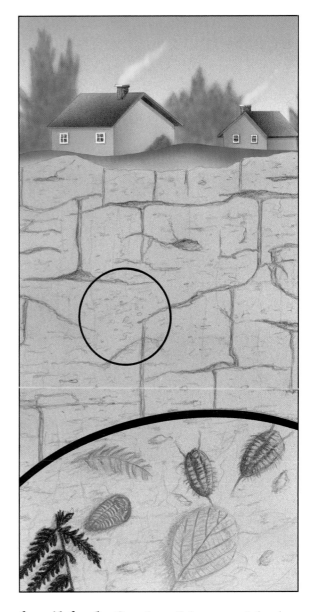

forest A large area of land covered mostly by trees growing close together along with other plants. There are many different kinds of forests, including rain forests, oak forests, pine forests, and mixed forests.

fossil fuel Combustible materials that formed beneath the ground over millions of years from the decayed remains of ancient plants and animals. Coal, oil, and natural gas are examples of fossil fuels. They are called nonrenewable resources because it takes millions of years to replace them.

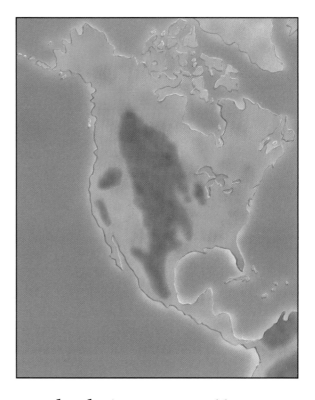

global warming A theory that the Earth is gradually becoming warmer because of an increase in the greenhouse effect. Some scientists think that the global temperature may increase anywhere from 2 to 9 degrees Fahrenheit by the year 2050, and cause great changes in climate and weather around the world.

fungus Any of a group of nongreen organisms that generally get the nutrients they need from dead or decaying organisms. Fungi (plural of fungus) include mushrooms, toadstools, yeasts, mildews, and molds. Some kinds of fungi can grow on living animals and plants and can cause many plant and animal diseases and a few diseases in humans such as athlete's foot.

grassland An area covered by grasses. In places where rainfall is abundant, trees grow intermixed with tall grasses. In drier places, only tall grasses grow. In semiarid regions, short grasses grow in bunches. Names for various grasslands around the world are prairies, pampas, savannas, and desert grasslands.

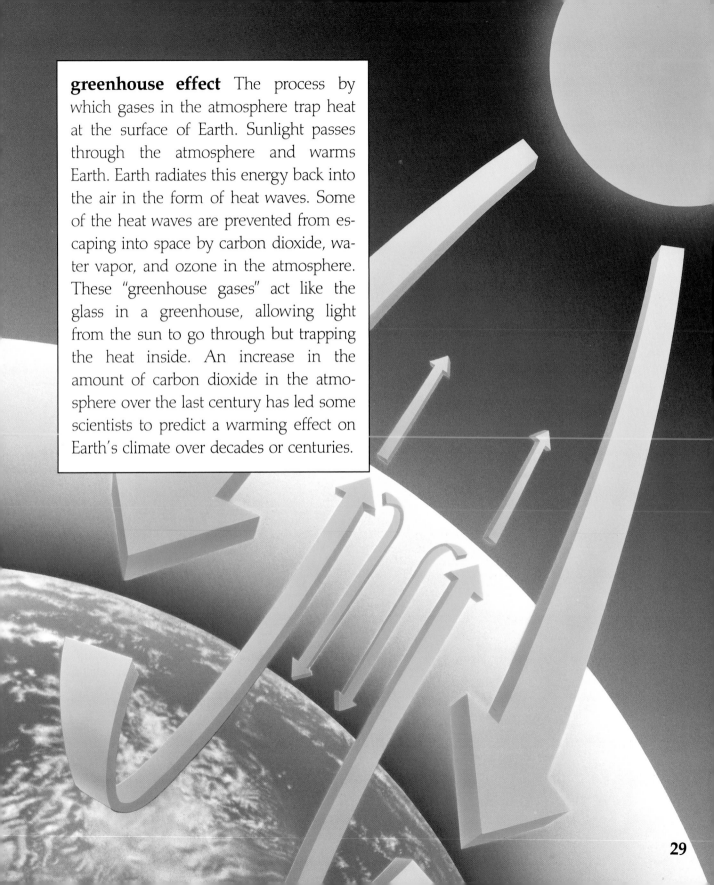

greenhouse effect The process by which gases in the atmosphere trap heat at the surface of Earth. Sunlight passes through the atmosphere and warms Earth. Earth radiates this energy back into the air in the form of heat waves. Some of the heat waves are prevented from escaping into space by carbon dioxide, water vapor, and ozone in the atmosphere. These "greenhouse gases" act like the glass in a greenhouse, allowing light from the sun to go through but trapping the heat inside. An increase in the amount of carbon dioxide in the atmosphere over the last century has led some scientists to predict a warming effect on Earth's climate over decades or centuries.

habitat A place such as a pond, or a grassy field, or a pine forest, where certain plants or animals live. The habitat includes all the environmental conditions in that place. Habitats can be small or large, depending on the plant or animal. For example, a wolf's habitat may spread for hundreds of miles, whereas some insects may live within a few square feet.

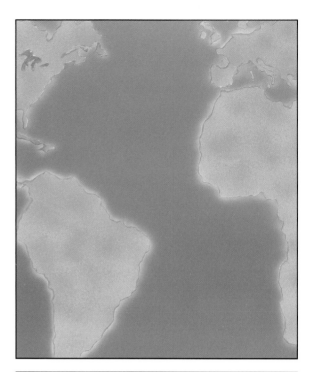

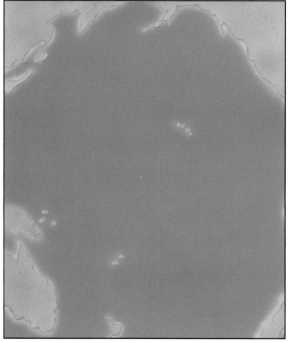

herbivore An animal that feeds upon plants or plant matter. Sheep, deer, and grasshoppers are examples of herbivores.

hydrosphere All the waters of Earth, including oceans, rivers, lakes, streams, and water vapor.

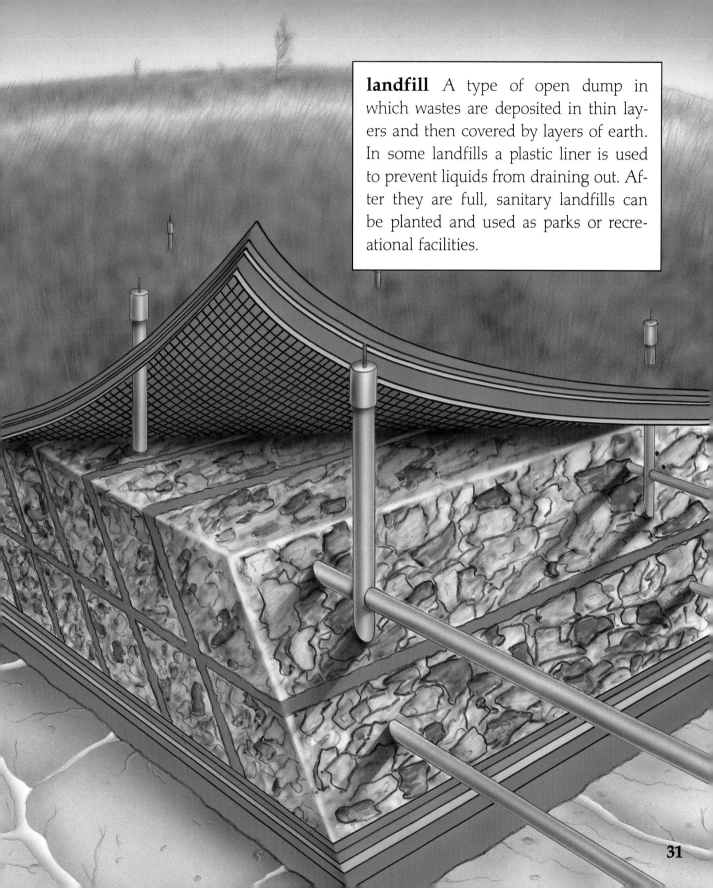

landfill A type of open dump in which wastes are deposited in thin layers and then covered by layers of earth. In some landfills a plastic liner is used to prevent liquids from draining out. After they are full, sanitary landfills can be planted and used as parks or recreational facilities.

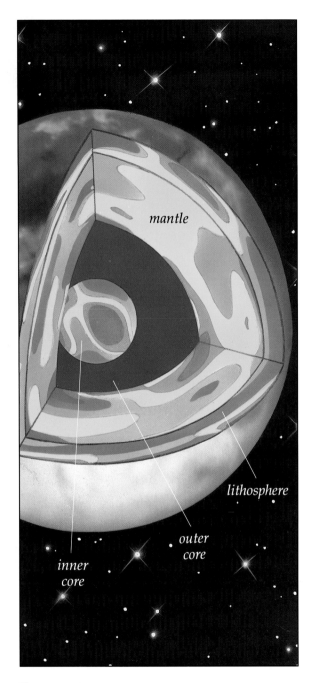

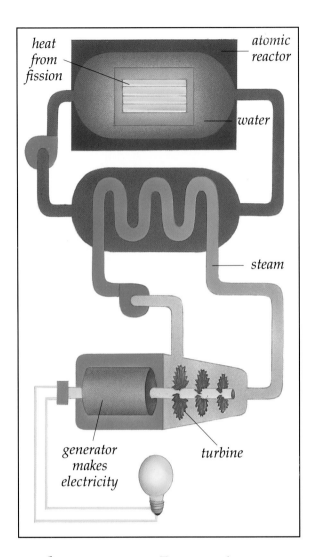

lithosphere The solid, rocky layers of Earth. The lithosphere includes the crust upon which we live and the top part of the mantle, the layer of rock that lies between the crust and the core.

nuclear energy Energy that is released when atoms of uranium or plutonium are split in an atomic reactor. This process is called atomic fission. Fission reactors have many drawbacks as a major source of energy, including the problem of safely disposing of their dangerous radioactive wastes.

nutrient A substance that is needed for the growth of a plant or animal.

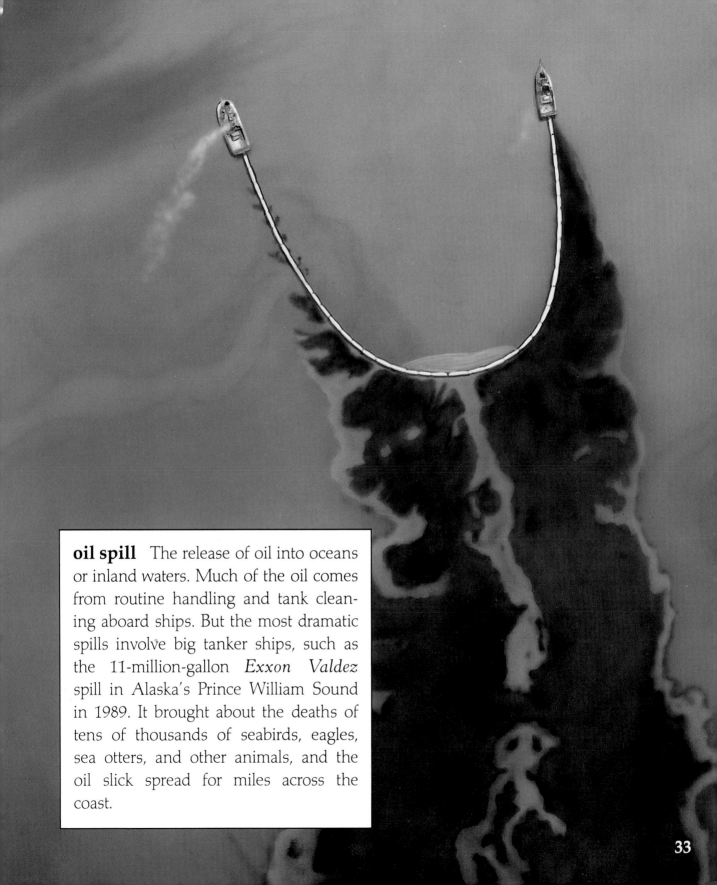

oil spill   The release of oil into oceans or inland waters. Much of the oil comes from routine handling and tank cleaning aboard ships. But the most dramatic spills involve big tanker ships, such as the 11-million-gallon *Exxon Valdez* spill in Alaska's Prince William Sound in 1989. It brought about the deaths of tens of thousands of seabirds, eagles, sea otters, and other animals, and the oil slick spread for miles across the coast.

omnivore Animals that eat both other animals and plants. Humans and bears are omnivores.

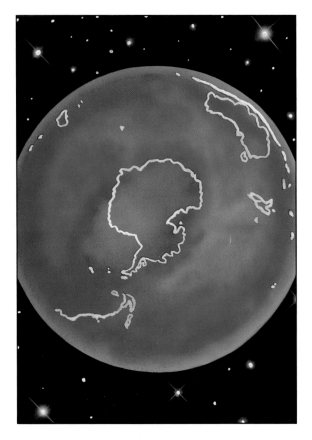

ozone layer Ozone is a form of oxygen that is mostly found in a layer of the upper atmosphere. The ozone layer protects life on Earth by filtering out UV (ultraviolet) and other kinds of harmful radiation. Scientists fear that gases such as CFC's (chlorofluorocarbons, chemicals found in refrigerators and air conditioners) are causing big holes to appear in the ozone layer over the Arctic and Antarctic. The holes expose life on Earth to dangerous levels of radiation.

PCB's A group of very poisonous chemicals (PCB stands for polychlorinated biphenyls) once widely used in the manufacture of plastics, as lubricants in industry, and in electronics. PCB's were released into the environment when factories poured their waste waters into streams and rivers. Once in the water, the PCB's were eaten by fish and shellfish and were passed along the food chain to humans who ate the fish. Even though the manufacture of PCB's was banned in 1979, they are still found in places where they were dumped and in animal tissues.

pesticide A substance that is used to kill plants or animals thought to be harmful to humans or human activities. Pesticides include herbicides that kill or stunt the growth of unwanted plants such as weeds; insecticides that are used to control mosquitos or other harmful insects; and germicides that kill harmful bacteria. Some chemical pesticides, such as DDT, can contaminate air, water, or soil and may harm humans and animals.

OXYGEN

CARBON DIOXIDE

WATER AND NUTRIENTS TRAVEL THROUGH ROOTS TO LEAVES

LEAVES CREATE FOOD WHICH IS STORED IN PLANT

SOIL NUTRIENTS

WATER

photosynthesis The process by which plants and bacteria use the energy of sunlight to make food. Green plants contain chlorophyll, a natural substance, which is able to use the sun's energy to combine carbon dioxide and water to make sugar. Oxygen is released by plants during photosynthesis.

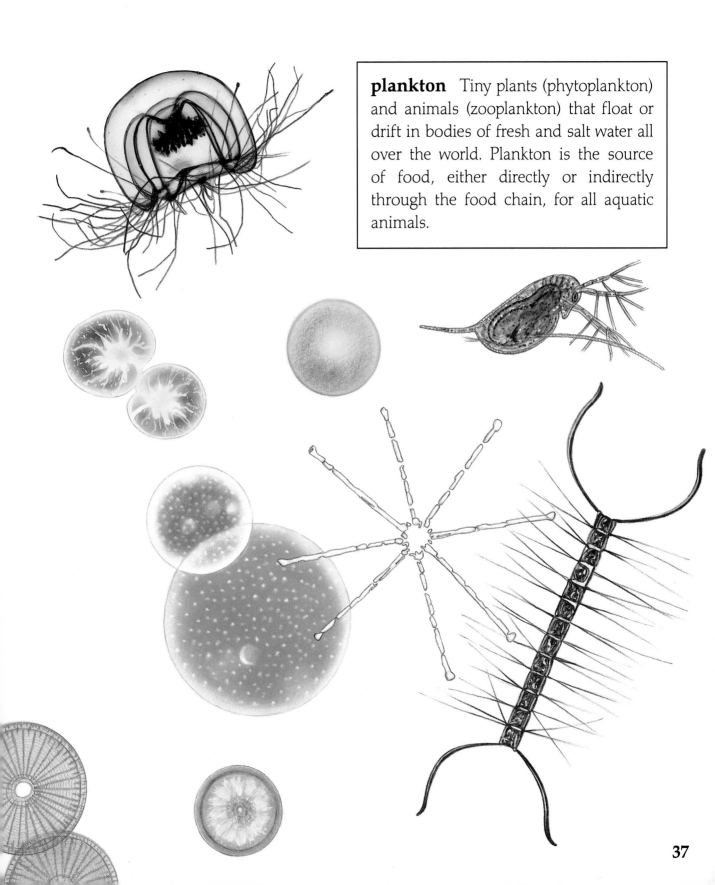

plankton Tiny plants (phytoplankton) and animals (zooplankton) that float or drift in bodies of fresh and salt water all over the world. Plankton is the source of food, either directly or indirectly through the food chain, for all aquatic animals.

37

pollution The presence or release of substances or waste heat into the air, water, or land that cause unwanted changes to the environment. The harmful substances are called pollutants.

pollution, air Air pollution, such as smog and acid rain, is caused by harmful gases given off by automobiles and factories. It can affect people's health, safety, and comfort. Air pollution was first noticed in the smoke of coal-burning factories built in the 1800's, but it was only in recent times that it came to be viewed as a major threat to health.

pollution, thermal The release of heated water from factories or power plants into a body of water. Because some animals and plants are sensitive to heat, even small amounts of excess heat from thermal pollution can harm organisms in the water. Thermal pollution can be controlled by cooling the water before it is released.

pollution, water The release of untreated sewage, industrial wastes, or poisonous materials into surface or groundwater. Polluted water can kill plants and animals that live in it, and harm people who drink it.

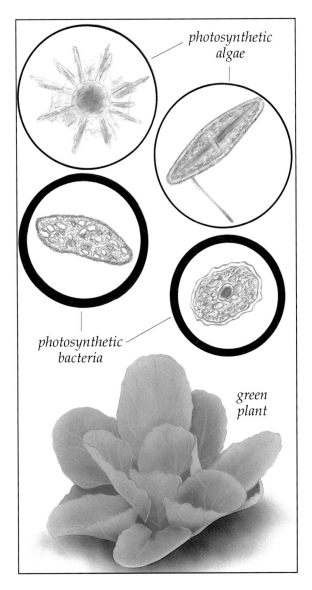

photosynthetic algae

photosynthetic bacteria

green plant

primary producer A living thing that is able to make its own food, from energy from the sun and water and carbon dioxide, through photosynthesis. Green plants, algae, and certain kinds of bacteria are primary producers. They provide food for all other kinds of living things. A primary producer is also called an autotroph (which means self-feeder).

radiation, atomic Energy produced from the splitting of atoms, most commonly uranium and plutonium. This energy is harmful to all living things. In some cases radioactive substances can remain harmful for thousands of years.

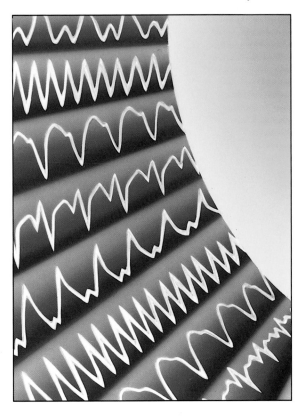

radiation, solar Energy given off by the sun in the form of heat, light, radio waves, and other kinds of energy, such as infrared radiation and ultraviolet light. Infrared radiation is heat waves that carry the sun's heat to Earth. Ultraviolet (UV) light is invisible to the eye but in large amounts is dangerous to life. The ozone layer protects Earth by absorbing these harmful UV rays.

rain forest A region of large, heavily overgrown trees and other plants where rainfall is very heavy. Rain forests are usually found in warm climates such as the Amazon River Basin or the islands of the South Pacific, but cooler-climate rain forests grow along the northwest coast of the United States. Many different types of plants and animals live in rain forests. Rain forests are considered an important resource to protect because of the large amounts of carbon dioxide they absorb from the atmosphere and the great variety of plants and animals that live there. If the amount of carbon dioxide in the air were to increase, the greenhouse effect would be much greater and the world's temperatures would rise.

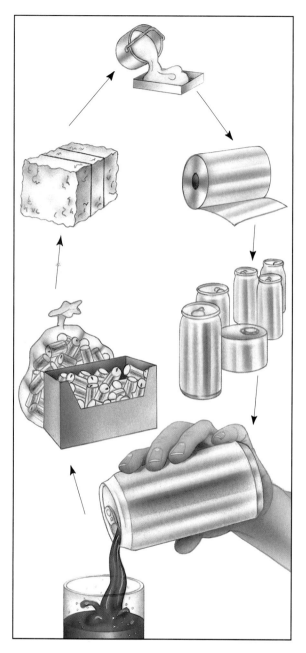

recycling A process by which glass, plastic, metal, paper, and other *wastes* are transformed into new products that can be used again. Recycling is one important way of dealing with the growing problem of waste disposal.

red tide A red color that sometimes appears at the surface of seawater that is caused by a sudden and abundant growth of a certain kind of plant plankton. The plankton produce a poisonous substance that can cause massive fish kills. While red tides can occur naturally, some may be triggered by nutrients dumped into the water by people.

sewage Liquid and solid wastes carried off in water that is channeled into the ground or into rivers or the ocean. In many cities, sewage is collected at a water-treatment plant, where the wastes are removed from the water and concentrated into a material called sludge.

smog A kind of dense, visible air pollution caused by automobile exhausts or the massive burning of coal and oil fuels. Smog can irritate eyes and lungs and be dangerous to people with respiratory illnesses. It can also damage buildings and other structures.

solar energy Energy given off by the sun. Solar energy is used by green plants for photosynthesis. The energy in fuels such as coal, oil, and wood comes originally from the sun, but there is a limit to the amount of these fuels, and burning them creates pollution. People are experimenting with devices that can directly change solar energy into usable forms of energy, such as electricity from solar batteries or solar heating in houses. Solar energy is nonpolluting and limitless.

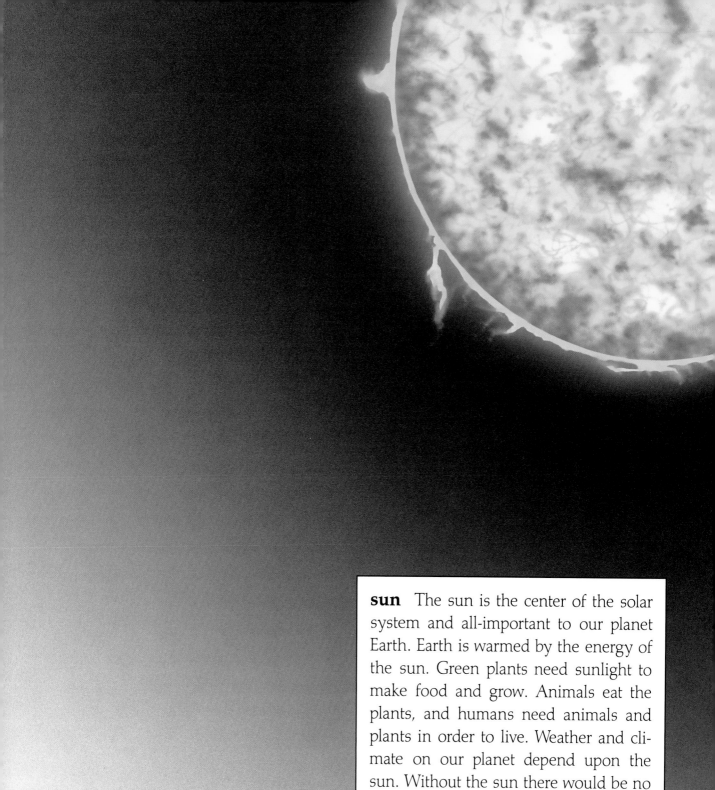

sun The sun is the center of the solar system and all-important to our planet Earth. Earth is warmed by the energy of the sun. Green plants need sunlight to make food and grow. Animals eat the plants, and humans need animals and plants in order to live. Weather and climate on our planet depend upon the sun. Without the sun there would be no life on Earth.

toxic Describing a substance that is poisonous or harmful to life. Pesticides and some chemical pollutants are toxic.

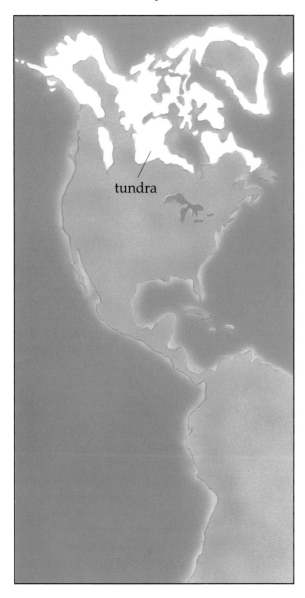

tundra A treeless plain found in arctic and subarctic regions. Just below the surface of the tundra is a subsoil called the permafrost, which is frozen hard throughout the year.

waste Unwanted substances that result from manufacturing or other human actions. Waste disposal has become a major problem because of the growing population and new kinds of dangerous wastes produced by industry. Examples of waste include raw sewage, garbage, toxic or poisonous chemicals, medical wastes, and radioactive wastes. The disposal of wastes from nuclear power plants is particularly important, because they may remain radioactive for thousands of years. Radioactive wastes are presently stored in metal and concrete containers in deep underground caves or old salt mines.

water cycle The continual circulation of water through the air across the land and into the oceans. Heat from the sun evaporates some water from oceans, other bodies of water, and the soil. In the atmosphere, water vapor condenses to form clouds and falls as rain or snow. Water flows over the surface of the land, and some of it returns to lakes, rivers, and the sea. Animals take in some of the water when they drink or eat and return water to the atmosphere when they breathe, perspire, or excrete. Leafy plants absorb water through their roots and return water to the atmosphere through openings in their leaves.

water-treatment plant A place where water can be cleaned. Water-treatment plants are designed to kill harmful organisms, remove suspended materials and unwanted minerals, and make the water fit for drinking and other uses.

wetland An area or a region that is usually wet or flooded, such as a marsh or swamp. Wetlands act as natural flood controls and are important natural habitats for all kinds of wildlife.